MEET ME IN MIAMI

1,000 Deliveries in the Magic City

Charles St. Anthony

THE CONTENTS

DEDICATION

This book is brought to you by the sponsors who contributed to the Miami Book Project GoFundMe. I give a heartfelt thank you to:

William and Patricia Ayres

Cydonie Fukami

Christine Johnson

Marcella Hammer

Lorna Handa

Christine Kawaguchi

Todd Phillips

Elizabeth Shoemaker

Emmie Smith

As well as several sponsors who wish to remain anonymous.

And of course, I always thank Judy Itoh for the encouragement.

THE MUSIC BROUGHT ME THERE

"Florida. The Spirit says go to Florida," said Gabrielle.

I had decided to leave Los Angeles but was not altogether sure where I wanted to go. Looking for an outside opinion, I consulted a Tarot Card reader in California's Venice Beach. Florida was not even on my radar. Besides the non-stop stories of strange crimes in the news, I felt wary of Florida's present politics. On top of that, I didn't think it wise to make major life decisions based on something flimsy like fortune-telling.

Was the Voice of Divine Inspiration truly whispering into Gabrielle's ear that I should go to an oddly shaped peninsula 2,700 miles (4,345 km) away? It's possible. I believe some things are beyond human comprehension. Maybe some people can decipher messages from beyond our plane of existence. Or maybe Gabrielle just wanted to go to Florida herself. She was reading Tarot in Venice Beach after all, so I would guess she had an affinity for sunny beach locations. Despite the bad press Florida gets these days, between the weather and the entertainment, it seems many Americans still like to visit Florida, if only for recreation.

After leaving Los Angeles, I went to Oklahoma (which you can read about in *Saints & Sinners in Oklahoma City*). I made some amazing friends and uncovered a lot of hidden gems OKC had to offer. After a year there, I felt the tide was high enough to push onward. The next city I had intended to challenge was New Orleans. Between the food and the history, the book had half written itself. However, New Orleans is currently the "Murder Capital of America." Though millions of people go about their day in The Big Easy without getting murdered, I thought that the type of research I do, which involves driving about unfamiliar neighborhoods, would be ill-advised. I had to file Bourbon Street and its environs into the "not right now" cabinet of my brain.

As I packed to leave Oklahoma, I had an epiphany. I heard a friend I played with in the school band had passed away. He was on trumpet while I was on saxophone. I remember him to be a funny and amiable character. But he had died—a death brought on by entirely natural causes—and it hit home to me. Now, at the age of 45, I could die of something natural, and though it would be extremely unfortunate, it would not be altogether unheard of.

Where do I want to go? What do I want to be doing? If there was somewhere I wanted to go in this lifetime and something I wanted to do, ***I needed to be doing it now.***

So I took to listening to different online radio stations throughout the USA, and I thought that the city whose radio station I liked the most would be the place I would go. I considered Portland. I liked its laid-back, progressive vibe. Also, New York City still has a hold on my heart. But the online radio stations that I kept coming back to ended up being Miami's. The music they have on air has a lot of upbeat tempos. Whether it is the dance beats thumping in *reggaeton* or just good old dance music from back in the day generally, I could enjoy whatever station I listened to. I figured if I could agree with the citizens of Miami about music, then I would at least have that to build on.

Having gradually reduced all my possessions to just a suitcase and a few carry-on-sized bags, I waved goodbye to Oklahoma and set off south through Texas. For a split second, I thought I would be lazy and write my next book in Dallas. Florida was far away and Dallas was right there. Then I arrived in Dallas and saw the traffic there. After seeing freeways that looked like the 7th Level of Hades, I said, "What is this ungodly Hellscape?" I just kept pushing toward Florida.

I ventured south through Louisiana and psyched myself into a state of terror as I entered Mississippi. I enjoy listening to true crime podcasts, and as I crossed the border into Mississippi from Louisiana, a podcast about someone getting murdered in Mississippi came on. It was a complete coincidence, but after hours on the road, my imagination got the best of me. The highways seemed darkly lit, and the woods that surrounded the desolate highway seemed to hide dastardly secrets. Secrets that only end up as a murder episode on the *Crime Junkie* podcast.

After rocketing through the Deep South, signs in Alabama signaled Florida was growing close. I heaved a sigh of relief after I arrived in Florida after driving all night through Louisiana, Mississippi, and Alabama.

I felt I had not only crossed into a new state but into a different country. The low sea level and the subtropical climate mean the flora and fauna differ from not only the South but the rest of the United States as well. The greenery was lush and the humid air was refreshing and easy to breathe. I stopped to spend the night with a friend in the capital, Tallahassee.

Most people don't realize just how long Florida is. A drive from Tallahassee south through Orlando and down to Miami was still a good 500 miles (805 kilometers). I knew if I pushed myself, I could make it down to Miami for Halloween.

A WOBBLY WELCOME

As I drove south through Florida, I was still a couple hours from Orlando, the orange oil change light flickered on. Fortunately, the Chevy Trax made it down to Orlando, but I needed to spend the night as places offering oil changes had all closed for the night.

Did I need to go all the way down to Miami? Miami, as online forums warned me, was full of insane traffic, insane prices, and requires a grasp of Spanish which I struggle to speak. Orlando seemed safe. Orlando seemed sensible. But when did I ever do safe and sensible? What kind of book would safe and sensible make?

I flipped on my UberEats to try out delivering an order in Orlando. Within minutes, I got an order from Pizza Hut. I made $2.71, and the cheapskate heffa did not leave a tip. *Pocahontas and Goofy can keep Orlando*, I thought as I set the Google Maps destination to South Beach.

My heart beat faster with anticipation as I continued down the freeway. I had never been to Miami before, but its reputation from the '90s was still embedded in my mind.

There was a time when Miami was the white-hot epicenter of all that was fabulous. *Details* magazine would devote pages upon pages to dazzling nightclubs like Liquid. Run by glamour lesbian Ingrid Casares, Liquid's guest list was like a Who's Who of '90s luminaries. Was Club Liquid still open? Would Madonna or one of the Versaces still be there—I mean, Donatella is probably busy in Italy or whatever, but maybe Bobo Versace or some lesser Versace? Maybe I could finagle my way onto a yacht party with J. Lo or Bad Bunny or something equally thrilling. Surely I could find a way to rep the 305 with Mr. Worldwide—otherwise known as Pitbull—on a boat somewhere.

I made it to Miami Halloween night, which fell on a Monday. I pulled off the highway near downtown Miami into the wrong neighborhood. I should have just stayed on the freeway till I got to South Beach, but I was tired of the traffic and the incessant honking. Homeless men knocked on my windshield on dimly lit streets demanding cigarettes as I meandered about trying to find my way over the causeway to South Beach. It was apparent that no Versaces would be greeting me in this stretch of downtown Miami, where unsightly government offices loomed like Communist barracks in Soviet-era Vladivostok. *I hate this. I want to leave.* I thought briefly about returning to Pocahontas and Goofy in Orlando.

Finally finding my way over to the Macarthur Causeway, I zipped over to South Beach on the evening of Halloween 2022. Parking in South Beach is like the *Hunger Games*— street signs that threaten to slap you with a fine and tow your car line every street in Miami Beach.

Finally parking along Collins Avenue, I paid about $12 for just a few hours of parking and looked for some frivolity and mayhem to enjoy.

Time was still about 8 p.m., so I decided to try a pizza shop on a side street. Alas, I spent $15 for a piece of flat cardboard and dreary cheese. A hip Latin guy lured me into a swanky but empty bar patio saying it was still Happy Hour, and I could get 2 for 1 margaritas. Happy Hour margaritas still cost $25 a piece, so I wasn't that happy. I left without ordering.

I walked past the old Versace mansion which has been converted to a restaurant, and searched for these amazing clubs and bars that surely awaited my discovery. This is how I found out that South Beach on a weeknight might not get going until 1 a.m.

A few party kids roamed around—notably one man dressed as a skeleton with an extra bone in his costume attached to his crotch region. Though society had returned to a semblance of normalcy, had the pandemic put a damper on SoBe? In that particular moment, South Beach didn't feel fabulous and certainly not the homosexual Shangri-la I had anticipated.

"Do you know where Club Liquid is?" I asked some partiers in their 20s. They pranced down the sidewalk in some Party City animal ears and barely-there outfits.

"Club what?" said a woman wearing cat ears and a sparkly miniskirt. A fake eyelash was coming off, and it looked like a caterpillar was attacking her face. In her black stilettos, she wobbled like she had one too many strawberry daiquiris.

"Club Liquid."

"Oh, that's been closed for years. I think my aunt used to party there forever ago," replied a man in some devil's horns while he adjusted his pointy, red tail. "It was over by Lincoln Road. I think it's a Chick-fil-A now."

"No, it's a Walgreens," a brunette in fox ears corrected him. They wobbled away in the opposite direction.

My first impression of South Beach was that it felt overpriced, chintzy, and slightly downmarket. *Is this as good as it gets?* I thought to myself. *Maybe it's just an off night... On Halloween.*

That being said, my expectations were so high for Miami that only Gloria Estefan twerking with Ricky Martin on top of a megayacht disco ball would have satisfied me. *The Assassination of Gianni Versace*, a series produced by Ryan Murphy about the untimely demise of the fashion designer, made Miami look like it had a lengthy row of cute gay bars overlooking the ocean. Currently, there is one gay bar on the beach and a few more several blocks away. Nothing I would write home about. Dare I say it? The gay scene in Miami has become dull. Why did a serial killer get to have more fun in Miami than I did? Maybe I just didn't have an invitation to the right parties, but as a casual observer, the South Beach scene felt lackluster. It had a lot of extremely beautiful people with their noses in their phones slowly sipping $25 cocktails.

I was out way too early anyway. After driving all the way from Oklahoma, I felt too tired to be out any longer. I'd need to swing from the chandeliers some other night. I searched Airbnb for a reasonable place to stay. I found out that most Miami Airbnbs would try to pull a fast one by listing rooms for a low price like $25 per night, but they would actually be $225 per night. That's because Miami's Airbnbs try to spring a $200 cleaning fee on you as you finally book a room. I didn't realize this before I arrived, and now I found myself priced out of every Airbnb in Miami.

This made staying in Miami for any extended period a difficult venture, but I was determined to make it work. I bounced between hostels and the occasional Airbnb. I even applied to work at one hostel that advertised a volunteer program that allowed for free room and board in exchange for work. They didn't call back, and I realized my age and lack of Spanish probably prevented them from hiring me. I tried sleeping in my car, but it was too hot and too noisy. One night, desperate to lay down to sleep, I booked an hourly motel in Little Havana for four hours just to get some rest. I woke up four and a half hours later to a Cuban woman screaming at me on the phone that I had overstayed.

Exhausted, desperate, and with nowhere to stay I drove around trying to make enough money via UberEats and DoorDash to stay for the night. I only had $20 left, and I hadn't eaten anything that day. Would I try sleeping in my car again? Would I have to pull out a sleeping bag on the beach and pray a blue-leg hermit crab didn't snip my nose off as I slept? This Miami misadventure was turning out to be a complete and total disaster.

My phone rang. "Hi, this is Sebastian from the Mar Vista Hostel."

"I'm sorry?"

"You've been selected for our volunteer program. Where are you staying right now?"

Let's give Miami a chance, I thought. *By the Power of Shakira*, I held aloft my Chevy Trax key, *Miami show me your wonders!*

I spun the Chevy Trax around and headed back to South Beach. I had found a home in Miami.

LA FLORIDA

"**S**ail south until the butter melts, then turn right," goes the old saying that brought the Europeans to the New World. Twas the path Christopher Columbus followed in 1492 across the Atlantic which led him to the Bahamas, Cuba, and Hispaniola. Though the historical record is fuzzy, it is thought that Ponce de Leon joined Columbus on his second venture to the Americas in 1493. Acclaim for Ponce's military ventures back in Spain helped him land the position of first governor of Puerto Rico.

Christopher Columbus' son, Diego Colón, replaced him as Puerto Rico's governor forcing Ponce de Leon to look for another job. Being out of a job yet highly capable (I mean he was just governor), the Castilian royalty said unto Ponce de Leon, "Columbus Junior has got this Puerto Rican governor gig on lock. Just go do something else. Bimini? Yes, Bimini! Why don't you go look for Bimini!?" Bimini is a small island in what is now the Bahamas.

Searching for Bimini but discovering Florida, Ponce de Leon led the first *known* European expedition to what is now Florida in 1513. If you read about him in history class, textbooks used to say that Ponce de Leon was on a mission to find the Fountain of Youth. Groups of Native Americans greeted Ponce de Leon with spears and volleys. The Native Americans quite wisely ascertained that these explorers might not have their best interests in mind. At the time, the Spaniards' *modus operandi* was, "Since you don't believe in Jesus Christ, we'll just take all your gold." Is it any surprise the Seminoles didn't roll out the red carpet for Ponce de Leon?

On his second voyage to Florida, Ponce de Leon found himself even more ill-favored. Native Americans shot an arrow piercing his thigh, and he succumbed to the wound after his party decamped to Cuba. Ponce de Leon didn't even realize that Florida was part of a continent when he died. He thought Florida was another island in the Caribbean.

Reports of the search for the Fountain of Youth don't come into the historical record until decades after de Leon's passing. Hence, Ponce de Leon's search for the Fountain of Youth is historically tenuous at best and a steaming pile of drivel at worst. Ponce de Leon did leave with us the name for this oddly-shaped peninsula. He called it "La Florida," referring to the bountiful vegetation of the region he made landfall—likely just north of Daytona Beach. Additionally, La Florida is also referred to as "Pascua Florida" (Feast of Flowers), a Spanish term for Easter.

None of the European powers knew quite what to do with Florida. Though in a strategic position, it did not have much of the gold the Spanish were after, with early accounts describing Florida as, "full of bogs and poisonous fruits, barren, and the very worst country that is warmed by the sun."

The colonial powers played hot potato with Florida for centuries. The Spanish botched several attempts to settle in Florida and eventually founded St. Augustine in 1565. This city holds the distinction of being the oldest continuously inhabited European settlement in the contiguous United States. The French tried to get in on the action by sending their Protestants (Huguenots) over, but the Catholic Spanish viewed them as heretics and vanquished the French from Florida in short order.

Later, the Spanish chucked Florida over to the British after the Seven Years' War in 1763. The Spanish used Florida as a bargaining chip to get Cuba back—trade routes from the Caribbean made Cuba more important to the Spanish at the time. The British lobbed Florida back to Spain after losing the American Revolutionary War. It bears mentioning that Florida found itself on the wrong side of history several times, siding with the British during the Revolutionary War and with the Confederacy during the Civil War.

Possibly foreshadowing Florida's reputation for strange criminal activity, Florida became a haven for people on the run. British sympathizers, escaped slaves, and colonial good-for-nothings all made Florida their home before the United States annexed the region. Men known as *banditti* (bandits), would dash in and out of Florida and Georgia committing crimes and hiding out in the sparsely populated backwater. It wasn't until the late 1800s that Florida emerged as a tourist destination and spurred the development of Miami.

A BURGEONING METROPOLIS

There wasn't much to see in Miami before the railroads. Two female landowners hastened Miami's development by attracting the attention of a prominent railroad magnate. Julia Tuttle and Mary Brickell persuaded railroad tycoon Henry Flagler to bring his railroad down to what was then just a soggy, isolated village. A cold snap devastated the orange crop in most of Florida in 1894, but Miami's weather had still been warm. Ms. Tuttle sent Henry Flagler flowers—a bouquet that possibly contained orange blossoms—as evidence of the warm temperatures even in the winter months. The two women joined forces with an enticing offer of land for Henry Flagler, and the tycoon brought the first railroad down to Miami.

Since historical research is my passion, I dug deeper into the Flagler history. After hours upon hours of research deep in the bowels of the Miami-Dade Public Library, I have uncovered a top-secret telegram from Mary Brickell to Henry Flagler. Here for the first time ever, I am publishing the contents of the 1894 Brickell telegram:

> "Hey Henry (stop). Why don't you bring your choo-choo all the way down south (stop). I've got a patch you can lay your tracks down on (stop). Here in South Florida, we keep it sweaty all year round (stop). I've even got a special treat for you ... it's orange, it's firm, and if you peel the skin back and bite into it, it's a little bit sour and a little bit sweet (stop).
>
> Very truly yours,
>
> Mary 'the Minx' Brickell (full stop)"

Mary "the Minx" Brickell—Saucy Temptress and
19th Century Landowner

With the power of the railroad, the construction of grand hotels, and the adoption of indoor air conditioning, Miami blossomed as a tourist destination. Miami grew from a hamlet with a population of 5,000 in

1910 to a city of 110,000 in 1930. During Prohibition, Florida's complacent attitude toward alcohol and gambling drew an assortment of characters. Rumrunners smuggled cheap alcohol from the Bahamas and turned booze into gold until Congress repealed Prohibition in 1933. It is perhaps unsurprising that Miami held allure to gangsters such as Al Capone and gangster-adjacent types such as Frank Sinatra.

It would be impossible to describe the current city of Miami without mentioning the prevalence of the Cuban diaspora in the region. Situated a mere 103 miles (166 km) from the Florida coast, Cuba already had a great deal of commercial and cultural exchange with South Florida before Fidel Castro overthrew the Batista regime in 1959. In the two decades following Cuba's communist takeover, around half a million Cubans arrived in the Miami area, established businesses, and shaped the culture of the city. In 2014, *The Miami Herald* estimated the Cuban-born population of Miami to be 700,000 people, and Cuban-Americans comprise over half the population of Miami. The 2020 census estimates 72% of Miami's population to be Hispanic, 13.6% black, and 11.4% Caucasian.

Some people describe Miami as "The Capital of Latin America." I'm not sure I agree with this assessment. When it comes to finance, São Paulo and Mexico City might like a word. In the current world of Latin music, I would argue Puerto Rico and Colombia certainly upstage Florida's importance. There is no arguing, however, that Miami is a nexus where the cultures of North America and South America converge. You can flex your Spanish at many familiar American shops. You'll also be able to indulge in the savory delights of Latin America without ever reaching for your passport.

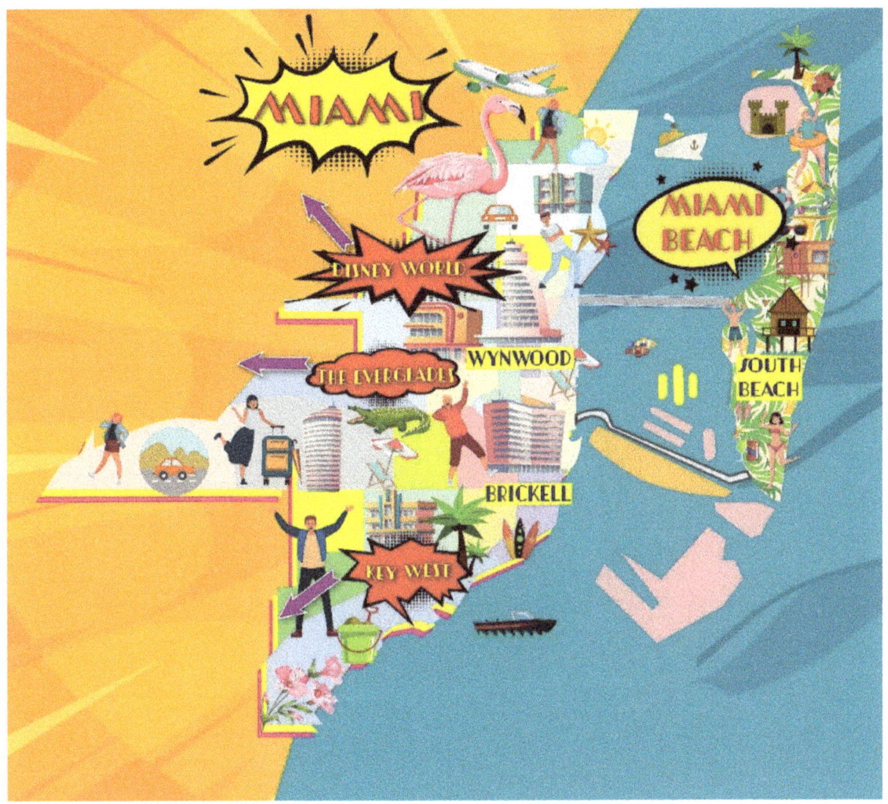

Many people who visit "Miami" are unaware that they might be spending only a small amount of time in the city of Miami itself. That's because the beach and nightlife area that most tourists stay in is centered on islands in the City of Miami Beach. Miami Beach contains the promenade and Art Deco district which people generally envisage when they think of Miami. Miami Beach connects to the mainland with a series of bridges and causeways.

One neighborhood worth mentioning is Brickell—named after the aforementioned Mary Brickell. This area contains many banks and businesses that make Miami a financial center. Honestly speaking, my first thought when visiting Brickell was: *Why would anyone want to come here? It's expensive, traffic is hellish, and you're not at the beach.* I have recently grown fond of Brickell's charms. It is one of the most walkable areas of Miami, and as months go by I increasingly find it an urban center with a fab factor that is distinctly Miami's own.

Another name that is on everyone's lips is Wynwood. In addition to festive nightlife, Wynwood contains several city blocks dedicated to street art and graffiti. While you are out enjoying the art and party scene, stop by the Wynwood Jungle—an atrium filled with shops and light installation artwork. At the Wynwood Jungle, you absolutely must try something at The Salty Donut, which is sort of a strange name since the donuts aren't salty. The Salty Donut sells sinfully delicious treats which include donuts like the Hazelnut + Chocolate, Banana Cream Pie, and the Maple + Bacon (yes, bacon).

FOODIE EXTRAVAGANZA!

In order to explore the culinary world of Miami, I have conducted more than 1,000 deliveries in the Miami metro. This includes 418 deliveries for data gathering purposes in which I accept every offer that pings me. I couldn't afford to keep accepting every offer after the first 400. *Meet Me in Miami* wasn't going to turn out very well if I starved. Also, this happened.

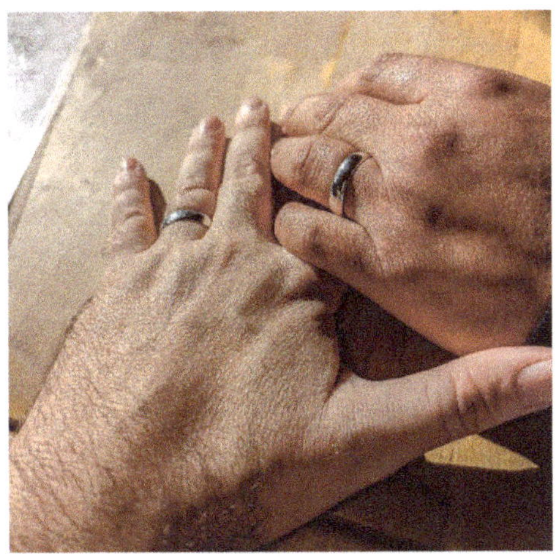

That's right. I got married. It turns out I picked up more than pizza in the Magic City.

While volunteering at the Mar Vista Hostel, I ran into a gentleman visiting the hostel in room #7, a Nicaraguan named George (Jorge). After several weeks of flirting and getting to know one another, I finally got his number while walking down Washington Boulevard in Miami Beach.

I'm a tightly wound creature who is prone to fits of nervousness. The hostel volunteer work was quite difficult for me as it involved trying to assist foreign visitors in my struggle Spanish. I was at the front desk reception looking down in frustration when I felt a hand rubbing my upper forearm. I looked up and George was smiling at me. George can calm me down with just a light touch and a warm smile. That's when I realized I wanted to marry him.

While volunteering at the hostel, I had to share a bunk bed with other volunteers. My volunteer work included some overnight shifts meaning I slept in during the day. George would visit the hostel while I was still sleeping and find a way to sneak into my room, shimmy up the bunk bed, and kiss me. Sharing a bunk bed in my forties was not something I had wanted, but George's attentions made it fun and romantic.

Well, being a newlywed, I needed to focus on other things. My data collection involves meticulously taking screenshots of each order and logging all the data in a spreadsheet. I had to stop the statistic collecting part of the research after 418 deliveries. The other 600 deliveries I did in Miami were to make money.

Speaking of money, I made the most money delivering pizza.

Types of Establishments

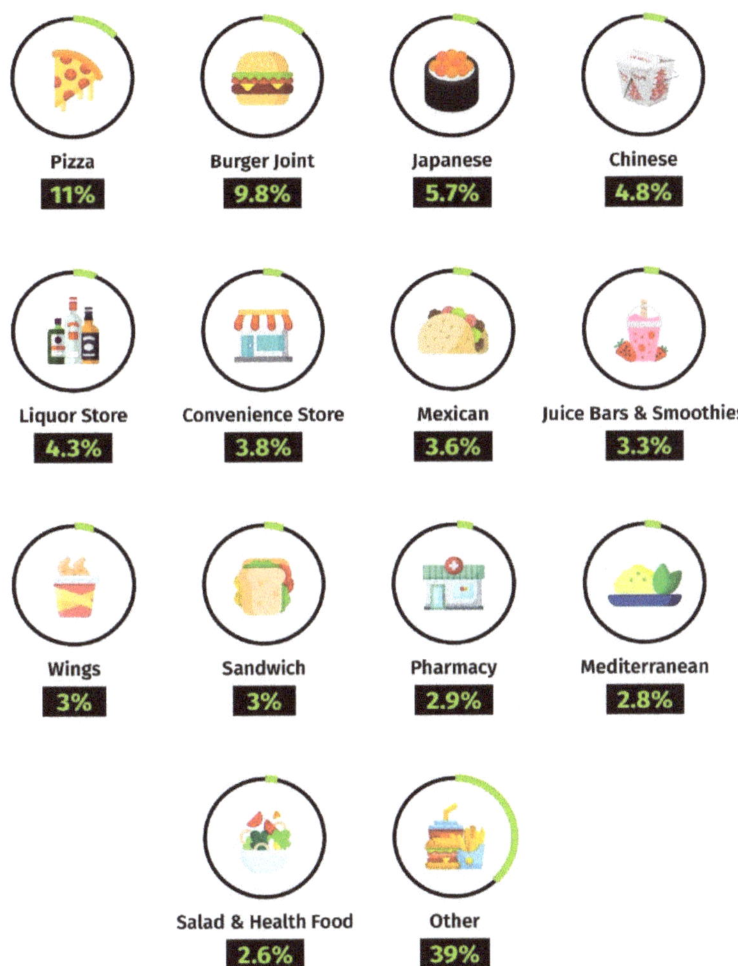

I would start my deliveries in Miami Beach and continue across the area taking one after another. Hence, half my deliveries for this project started in Miami Beach making this a case study not just of Miami, but of what people eat when they are on vacation. It turns out they eat pizza. Lots of it. 11% of the deliveries (47 orders) came from pizza joints. Pizza was the most popular category of food in this case study.

In Miami, pizza is followed in popularity by burger joint (9.8%) and Japanese food (5.7%). This contrasts my similar studies of Los Angeles and Oklahoma where the top three types of establishments were burger joint, Mexican, and chicken wings. In both LA and OKC, pizza was only fourth place, a mere 5% of the orders.

Most popular type of establishment

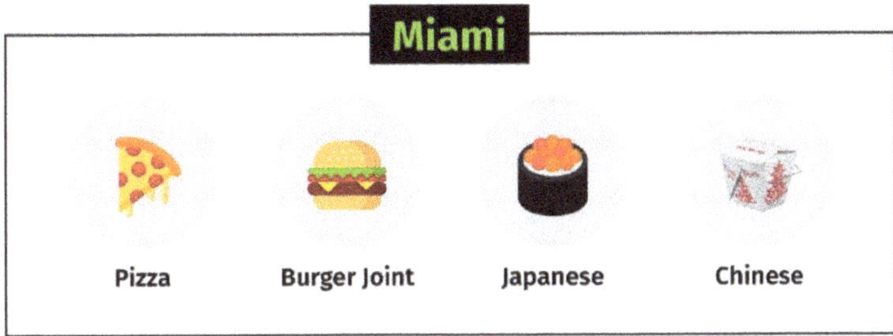

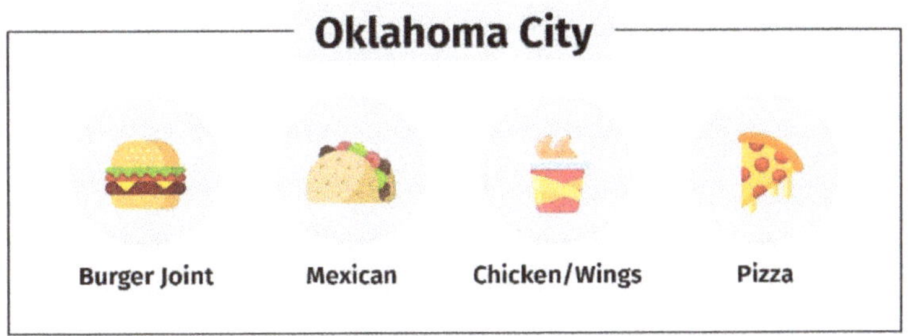

Though Miami's food preferences were unique, their taste in pizza was not particularly noteworthy. Pepperoni was the most popular topping with about ten pizzas topped with pepperoni in total—this includes three orders of the Shaq-a-roni from Papa John's. The Shaq-a-Roni is simply a very large pepperoni pizza with extra cheese and pepperoni. Basketball star Shaquille O'Neal is in the advertisements and apparently, the slices are "foldable." Most other orders were equally uninventive with orders for margherita, cheese, and Hawaiian pizza also in the mix.

That being said, there are some pizza delicacies to be had in Miami. The first one I'll introduce is from Spris Artisan Pizza. Spris operates five restaurants throughout the Miami area, and they boast an "Authentic Italian pizzeria cooked in our brick oven." In addition to Spris, I also recommend the "extraordinary" pizzas of Mister01. Many of the pizzas at Mister01 are named after people, with names like Luca, Beckham, and Carlos. I'm a sucker for a bit of truffle sauce, so I say treat yourself to a Star Alessandro pizza.

RUCOLA E PROSCIUTTO PIZZA

Ingredients: Arugula, prosciutto di parma.

STAR ALESSANDRO

Ingredients: ricotta cheese, mozzarella, ham, fresh tomatoes, roasted corn, black pepper, white truffle oil, basil.

EL SABOR LATINO

Every morning in Miami, you'll see men sipping their Cuban-style espresso. It comes prepared in little Dixie cups that you pour into paper shots. The paper shot cups look like the ones a pediatrician gives children to have some Robitussin, but the sweet espresso shots are much tastier than cough syrup. What makes it a *cafecito* (also called a *colada*) is the dark roast that's sweetened with brown sugar and topped with a delicious foam called *espumita*. I'm tempted to write a series of dirty jokes using the word espumita, but since I'm a conservative Republican woman just like Meghan McCain, I can't endorse such depravity. How you choose to guzzle Cuban espumita and lick it off your lips in the privacy of your own home is entirely up to you. I've been known to slurp up a bit of espumita myself from time to time, so I won't judge. Anyway, my favorite cafecitos were the ones served up by La Carreta in Little Havana.

Each of the nationalities that have established a foothold in Miami has created restaurants featuring their favorite dishes. My food research in Miami featured deliveries from Argentinian, Brazilian, Colombian, Cuban, Dominican, Honduran, Mexican, Nicaraguan, and Venezuelan restaurants. Various Latin American cuisines combined accounted for 13.2% or 56 of the deliveries. Many of them feature Latin American "home cooking" which is usually a plate dish of rice, beans, and some form of meat. A slice of avocado or plantains might accompany the dish. I'm embarrassed to admit that it took me almost a year of living here to find out what a plantain was. I had thought plantains were some exotic tropical plant that only grows atop trees in dense tropical rainforests. Something Sigourney Weaver might have discovered in *Gorillas in the Mist*. No, a plantain is similar to a banana and grows in many tropical countries. Plantains have a sweet taste rather than a banana taste, and many countries serve them fried.

If you want to try a typical Latin American plate dish, I recommend a *bandeja paisa* from Mi Colombia Cafeteria in Miami Beach. Should it be avocado season, the avocado is gratis! The staff is extremely friendly and there are signs on the wall informing you that the food is homemade and not just zapped in a microwave. If you need a refreshment, Mi Colombia's natural blackberry juice is refreshing as well.

A type of Latin treat I had never tried anywhere else is the *arepa*. This is a staple, particularly in Venezuela, and it looks like a sandwich made out of a pancake. The cornmeal dough has various fillings like a sandwich, but the dough isn't sweet like we serve an American pancake. You can try out arepas at Latin bakeries throughout the Miami area. A specialty restaurant called Doggi's Arepa Bar currently operates four locations throughout the Miami area. I enjoyed the Arepa Llanera which includes picanha steak, cheese, and a homemade chimichurri sauce.

Though I could write volumes about the delicious Latin foods available throughout Miami, I'll include just one more that I thought stood out. Should you be partying in Wynwood, I recommend you stop by La Tiendita Taqueria for a modern take on Mexican classics like *tacos al pastor* and *carne asada*. Sometimes you just need a good, solid taco. La Tiendita is along 25th Street off the main drag (NW 2nd Avenue) in Wynwood, and is a great place to get some solid Mexican food and a margarita during a night out in the party district.

BANDEJA PAISA

Ingredients: crispy pork skin, red beans, rice, fried eggs, sweet plantains, beef (grilled or ground)

AREPA LLANERA

Ingredients: grilled punta trasera (picanha steak), grilled cheese, and homemade chimichurri

CARNE ASADA TACOS

Ingredients: marinated grilled beef, guacamole, onion, cilantro

OTHER TREATS

The very first night I did deliveries, I got pinged from an innovative Japanese/Asian Fusion restaurant called "moshi moshi" in South Beach. The name itself, moshi moshi, is amusing because it's often how you answer the phone in Japan. They offer sushi and other tapas such as salmon sashimi tacos and crunchy crab ceviche. You place your orders through a QR code which directs you to a website—there's minimal interaction with the staff of moshi moshi. In my opinion, the must-try dish is the fried rice. The fried rice comes in varieties such as kimchi fried rice and shrimp fried rice, but this is Miami. Go big or go home—I recommend a dish called "moshi moshi fried rice" which mixes beef, chicken, pork, and egg in the rice. The establishment stays open until 5 a.m., and I hope you stumble into moshi moshi after one too many mojitos in Miami Beach.

My final two entries come from a notable foodie favorite called Blue Collar. North of downtown Miami along Biscayne Boulevard, you'll find the MiMo District from 50th through 77th Street. This stands for "Miami Modern" district, and you'll find a lot of remodeled deco-style hotels along with trend-setting foodie destinations. Blue Collar, an unpretentious comfort food eatery, has vegetable plates, grits, and "Cuban" spring rolls. The jalapeño cornbread is a showstopping menu item. Blue Collar's fresh-squeezed key lime pie is the stuff that dreams are made of. If I were to single out one dish out of everything I tried in Miami that you HAVE to try, it would be the cornbread at Blue Collar.

MOSHI MOSHI FRIED RICE

Ingredients: beef, chicken, pork, egg, carrot, lettuce, topped with scallions, sesame seeds

KEY LIME PIE

Ingredients: graham crust, vanilla whipped cream

JALAPEÑO CORNBREAD

Ingredients: cornbread, French sea salt, chile brown butter

TRENDS AND NUMBERS

To explore the culinary world of the Magic City, the data collection portion of the study included 418 deliveries in which I accepted every order that pinged me. I earned $2,570.84, with an average of $7.65 per delivery. As in other cities, I found UberEats to be busier while DoorDash compensates more per delivery. 342 UberEats deliveries averaged $7.70 per order while 76 DoorDash deliveries averaged $7.49.

As mentioned in the last section, pizza and Latin food proved more popular than in other regions of the United States. Another general trend I noticed was that non-pizza fast food establishments were less popular than in Los Angeles and Oklahoma. There are two factors that I believe contribute to this: 1. Lack of space, especially in Miami Beach, means less zoning for drive-thru establishments. 2. You need to look good for the beach, and you aren't going to do that by eating a lot of Burger King. You can't squeeze into a cute Speedo on a steady diet of Jack n 'the Box and Chick-fil-A. I mean, you could conceivably squeeze into the Speedo, I just can't tell you what the reaction would be.

Currently, the top three fast food establishments in the United States as a whole are as follows: McDonald's, Subway, and Taco Bell. McDonald's was the most popular in Oklahoma City with the Golden Arches accounting for 14% of my orders there. Los Angeles came next with 12% and McDonald's was the least popular in Miami, accounting for only 4.5% of my orders. Subway sandwiches had about the same popularity in all three cities accounting for 1 - 2% of the orders in all three. Taco Bell was more popular in Los Angeles (7% of the orders), followed by OKC (5.5%), and then Miami (2%).

Percent of People
Who Tipped

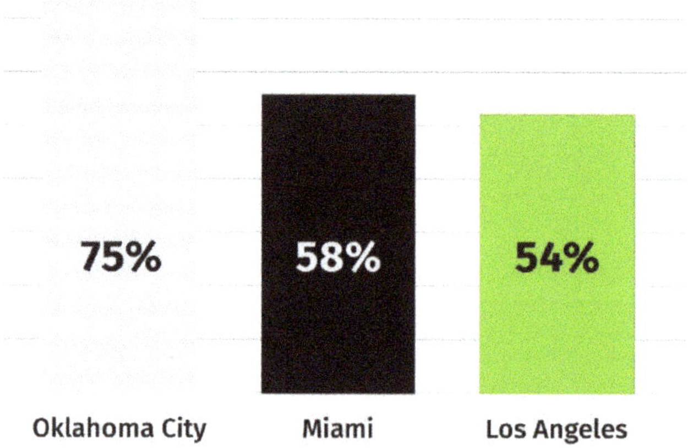

Average Tip

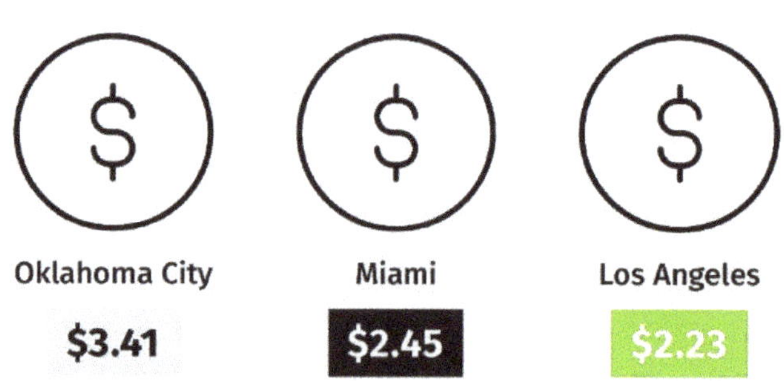

As for generosity, Miami sits in between the two cities. Miami was slightly more generous than Los Angeles—Miami residents tipped 58% of the time an average of $2.45, marginally higher than Angelenos who tipped an average of $2.23 54% of the time. The people of the heartland in Oklahoma City still beat them both by tipping an average of $3.41 75% of the time. I will say this in defense of my Angeleno brethren: I carried out that study during the thick of the pandemic, so people might have been feeling the pinch more than my other studies.

The total distance traveled during the data collection was 1,177 miles (1,894 km) with an average of 2.8 miles (4.5 km) per delivery. That makes the distance I drove during data collection 20 times the length of the Panama Canal or about half the length of the Oregon Trail.

As you might imagine, between moving across the country, working multiple jobs, getting married, and driving like a maniac, I am tired. So I'm going to rest my eyes for a second and allow you to peruse the facts of my extraordinary infographic.

Length traveled

 **1,177 miles (1,894 km)** 

- -

Average trip: 2.8 miles (4.5 km)

 **Trips to Liquor Stores** `18`

Orders of French Fries	Orders of Empanadas	Orders containing plantains	Orders of arepas
`54`	`7`	`4`	`4`

EVERYMAN
FOR THEMSELVES

This was almost the book that didn't get finished.
Both human and divine forces seemed to be working against me
every step of the way.

We are talking about Florida, which has become a national punchline
due to the bizarre occurrences that happen here with shocking fre-
quency. The "Florida Man" joke comes from the fact that if you enter
"Florida Man" into a Google News search, you are likely to find an assortment of strange articles about weird crimes and drugged-out she-
nanigans. Searching "Florida Man" now as I write this just brought up a
CNN article by the title "79-year-old hospitalized after alligator attack
at community golf course." Thankfully, this gentleman survived and
even joked, "Go figure. Out for a walk to stay healthy." Rather than getting in shape, he got attacked by a seven-foot reptile from a swamp.
Alligators seem to factor into a lot of Florida Man stories such as the

classic "Florida man threw live gator in Wendy's drive-thru window." He must have eaten a funky Baconator or something.

Other Florida Man stories seem to involve heavy narcotics use. For example, one story that garnered national attention was a horrifying story in which a man got high on bath salts, took his clothes off, and accused a homeless man of stealing his Bible. The Florida Man then partially ate the face of the victim. He growled at police when they tried to get him to stop. Tragically, the police shot him to stop the attack. Other notable headlines of Florida tomfoolery include:

"Florida man wearing 'No, seriously I have drugs 'T-shirt arrested for possession of drugs."

"Florida man drives stolen truck to Space Force base to warn of battle between aliens and dragons."

"Florida man charged for throwing hot dog at St. Pete officer."

I have a theory about Florida Man. Today Florida is populated by people with completely different motivations. The state contains a wide variety of people and cultures such as retired folk, Cubans, swamp-dwelling rednecks, and Jewish people. I'd also add that Florida is a state that many people flee to when they have problems elsewhere, such as those behind on child-support payments or struggling with other large amounts of debt.

Add to this mix the fact that Florida is a major port of entry of narcotics into the United States, and you have a recipe for some exceedingly bizarre situations. The inorganic nature of the mix of people and cultures—removed from whatever community they originally came from—bouncing off each other in an atmosphere peppered with drugs and extreme heat breeds Florida Man.

While living and working at the Mar Vista Hostel, the atmosphere of South Beach fostered crazed encounters. I encountered one such Florida Man incident during my first days working there. A Latin guy who looked to be in his thirties emerged from a second-story window of a building across the street from the hostel and began yelling, "Help! Help!" The man's skin glistened from drug-induced sweat and his eyes seemed to focus on something far in the distance. His matted black hair suggested a life in disarray.

I rushed over to see what I could do, and he kept screaming. As he attempted to climb down onto an awning he fell to the sidewalk smacking his head on the concrete. I called 911 hoping that they would put him in an ambulance, but the police cuffed him and put him in the back of a police car like a common criminal. A policewoman I spoke with later assured me they took him to a hospital, but the incident shook me nonetheless.

It was not entirely surprising to see something like this in South Beach, as the area itself is like an open-air drug market. Young people now get shot there every Spring Break, and if you walk around certain parts of the Boardwalk, people will offer a variety of chemical substances to purchase. I would highly advise against buying drugs off the street since they can be cut with dangerous additives such as fentanyl. People would regularly "tip" volunteers at the hostel with drugs rather than taking them on an airplane as they left Miami. When someone gave me a baggy full of MDMA I would immediately flush it down the toilet rather than ingesting the Molly. Since I'm gainfully employed at the moment, that is the story I'm sticking to.

The Mar Vista Hostel was located in a particularly seedy section of South Beach, and people would frequently get banned or removed for a variety of misbehaviors. That being said, the volunteers and staff themselves were part of the mischief. Indeed, one fellow volunteer, who shall remain nameless, would often wake me up by loudly snorting ketamine. I would rub my eyes, and he would be using the swivel part of his fingernail clippers to scoop up the powdery white substance and inhale it.

Veterinarians use ketamine as an anesthetic on animals, and this particular drug was popular with rowdy club-goers in the '90s. *What's going on here?* I would think. *Is my roomie planning on going to the Limelight? Should I get Amanda Lepore on the phone? Are we going to the Tunnel?* I would tune this commotion out and go back to sleep, as the roommate would drift into a K-hole.

In one incident we had a trans woman who was staying in the female dorm. She wasn't banned for being transgender, but because she went around bragging about how she had just been released from jail for theft. Other guests staying at the hostel suspected she was pilfering their belongings, as well. After being banned from the hostel, she would often hang outside the stoop of the hostel where riff-raff could be found, drinking and smoking at all hours of the day and night. The hostel did have a security camera system, so when she'd come back management would message me. I'd have to ask her to leave the premises. Eventually, she started calling me "faggot" and asking what I had against her. A trans woman calling a gay man a "faggot" is, well, a choice.

She strutted into the main lobby one night, and shouted, "I don't know what your problem is, faggot. Is it my beautiful body or perfect tits that's making you jealous?" She then flashed her breasts to all the on-lookers in the hostel. Her wonky boob job looked like she purchased her flapjack titties off a Groupon in a Hooverville, so no, I was not jeal-ous. *I just don't want to lose my job, since the management doesn't want you here.* She might have just said, "Excuse my beauty." Luckily, this gender-bending nightmare pranced off into the night without any police intervention.

I was not so lucky another night. It came to my attention that one guest might have been snuck into a room without paying. She was sum-moned to the front desk, and this woman started screeching and yell-ing. She had a right to be upset because it turns out this was a mistake on the part of one of the staff. She had paid for her stay. We didn't realize this in the moment, and she hurled abuse at me. Other staff were whispering for me to call the police. She accused me of calling her a rottweiler, said she would kill me, and then threatened to have me killed (which is sort of redundant if you think about it). The police came and a scene ensued. The men in blue escorted her out of the building along with her luggage.

They brought her back in briefly to ask if she could get her $20 deposit back, and that's when I turned into a Petty Patty and said, "When you threaten to kill the staff, you don't get your $20 deposit back." Buh-bye.

If you have a frenemy that is coming to Miami, you might suggest that they drive here! Tell the person you hate to scoot over to Hertz and check out their options. Out of every city I have driven in the USA, I would rank driving in Miami as the most unpleasant. Which is really saying something when you consider I've lived in San Francisco and Los Angeles. You are constantly being forced to merge, dodge some stupid trolley, and maneuver around construction. Drivers are in such a rush they will honk at you from behind even while pedestrians are walking in front of your car.

The Parking Gestapo regularly slaps you with a ticket at any chance they get, and the word on the street is they pay people to tip off the parking patrol should someone park illegally for a bit. Doing DoorDash and UberEats, parking is often not provided at places you pick up or drop off, so it becomes a game of "how many times can I park illegally and get away with it." It doesn't make financial sense to pay $2 to park when you are only making $4 for a delivery. One such delivery parking quagmire is at the TGI Friday's along Ocean Drive in South Beach, where there is usually no legal parking available for several blocks. I always had to park illegally in the alley behind Friday's. The operators of this establishment kindly note in the app that parking at Friday's is "Everyman for themselves."

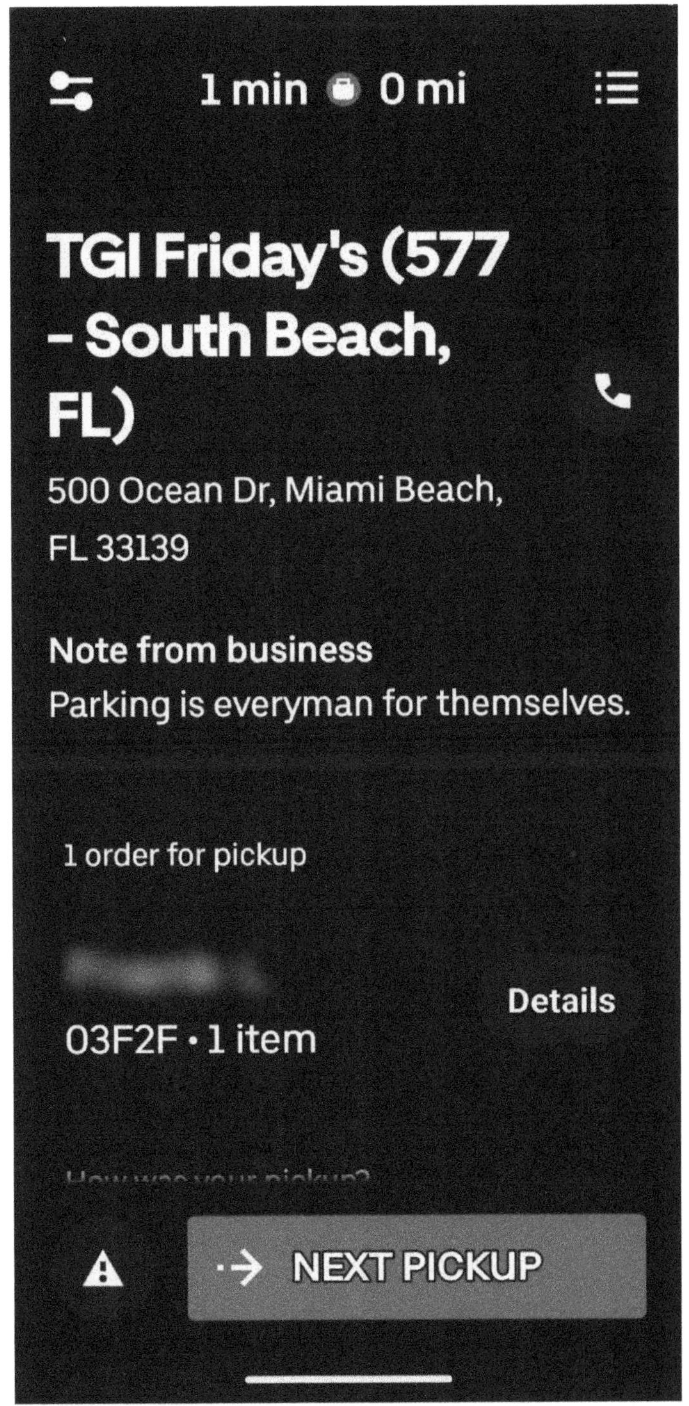
1 min 0 mi
TGI Friday's (577 - South Beach, FL)
500 Ocean Dr, Miami Beach, FL 33139
Note from business
Parking is everyman for themselves.
1 order for pickup
Details
03F2F · 1 item
How was your pickup?
NEXT PICKUP

People guard their legal street parking like hawks. Once I impinged on a gentleman's parking spot by six inches while picking up a delivery from Yambo Nicaraguan restaurant. He became aggressive and started pushing me when I came back out. I desperately tried not to drop the *gallo pinto* I was delivering as the man yelled, "You need to learn how to read! This is my spot!" And he's right. When will I learn how to read? Being illiterate has been challenging as an author. I'll get on that for him.

Sprinkled about the Miami region and all of South Florida are draw-bridges. Miami Dade County operates eight of these movable bridges, which are often located in major car traffic thoroughfares such as Brickell Avenue and the Venetian Causeway. Generally, you are stuck waiting in your car for five to ten minutes while a tugboat comes floating out. Turning lemons into lemonade, I usually have time to complete an entire Spanish Duolingo lesson while I wait for the drawbridge to come back down.

To put this in perspective, it would be like New York City shutting down 6th Avenue during rush hour to let a boat pass. It's a bane for deliveries since you might be delivering something that melts, such as ice cream. On the bright side, I can now fluently say "The crab drinks milk" (El cangrejo bebe leche) in Spanish due to the Duolingo lessons I completed while waiting for drawbridges—my Nicaraguan husband appreciates this immensely.

In addition to Florida Man, unruly hostel guests, and parking debacles, I suffered car problems throughout this time. Though I fancy myself as some sort of Hunter S. Thompson of the digital age and boasting a worldwide network of amazing readers (I love you), staying afloat financially has been a challenge. So halfway through this project, my whole life felt like it was being undone. My few possessions were all breaking or broken, and I was unable to seek medical attention because I was paralyzed with fear about how much it would cost—I was experiencing a very hand-to-mouth existence.

Still in the early stages of the project, my car battery died, forcing me to pull over on a busy section of Washington Blvd. on a Saturday night. I had needed a battery jump twice before, so it wasn't a complete surprise the battery went kaput. Luckily, my car insurance sent someone to help, and I thought my luck must be turning around. A beautiful Latin guy showed up. He was muscular, gorgeous, stylish ... and he ripped me off. He sold me a replacement battery that died two days later. My Chevy Trax sat unused on a side street of Miami Beach for almost a week before I had the money to have it towed to the shop. Paco at Autonation informed me the Adonis had sold me a bunk battery that was several years old.

Fortunately, I can say that the deliveries themselves went for the most part smoothly considering I've made more than 1,000 deliveries. It even got me learning more Spanish as I now know "pound on the door"

(Golpear la puerta) and "leave it at the door" (Déjalo en la puerta). No-table incidents while making deliveries were few and far between. One time, a wings place gave me the bag for a woman named Asia, but they had given my order to another woman named Asia. Neither of the two women named Asia was Asian. There was the occasional rude cus-tomer and the occasional stolen order, but doing the deliveries was the easy part. It's just the rest of everything in Miami that was a mess.

THE CHOICE TO STAY POSITIVE

I have now done similar studies across the entirety of the United States. I started my gig economy journey in San Francisco (chronicled in *Uber Diva*), did two studies in Los Angeles (*DTLA Hustler* and *Beverly Hills Postmate*), and brought my talents to the Great Plains (*Saints & Sinners in Oklahoma City*). More than five years have passed since I began my gonzo-style writing about gig work—partially spurred by intellectual curiosity, but also due to financial necessity. The gig work started before, was conducted during, and today continues after the coronavirus pandemic. Several establishments I introduced in Los Angeles shuttered their doors during the pandemic. In the meantime, I've held jobs, worked as an extra in a RuPaul movie, fallen in love, been inspired, been vaccinated, survived two car accidents, and motored all across the country. I have traveled more than 5,091 miles (8,193 km) doing deliveries and made $11,635.97.

Finally making my way over to Miami, I have made some amazing discoveries. Miami feels much like a foreign city in terms of food, language, and culture. Some of the little things that make Miami magical take a while to discover. I love the tiny lizards that scurry across the sidewalk. I know no other major US city where flocks of live hens and roosters camp out in the middle of the busy downtown. The lights, the music, and the dancing give the city a *joie de vivre* found nowhere else. I especially enjoyed one parking lot attendant in South Beach who would be booty shaking to Caribbean tunes when I arrived, and still be shaking it hours later when I came to pick up my car. You're not gonna see that in Schenectady.

Beautiful and chaotic, I am sorrowed when I think of how ephemeral this city and everything in it might be. Miami reminds me of the myth of the Lost City of Atlantis. The people of the legendary city were said to have been beautiful and fantastical. Technologically advanced and in control of a bountiful land, the Atlanteans succumbed to greed and avarice. The land was smitten by the gods and sunk beneath the ocean. Whether Plato intended his story of Atlantis as a historical fact or merely a metaphor for the hubris of mankind will continue to be debated.

While writing *Meet Me in Miami*, my heart hurts thinking this writing might end up being a record of a once fabulous city that no longer exists. The state of Florida, and in particular Miami, reminds me of the story of Atlantis. Here we have a city filled with gorgeous people and in possession of more technology and wealth than the ancients could have ever fathomed. Miami is fabulous and cosmopolitan and attracts excellence from across the world. When Shakira divorced, she could have left Spain for anywhere. She came to Miami. When Lionel Messi's soccer contract was up at Paris Saint-Germain, he could have played anywhere. He came to Miami. The city that attracts some of the world's most notable citizens is also Ground Zero for climate change.

Having grown up an environmentalist, I'm aware that many are sounding the alarm. According to *The Guardian*, scientists report that "the lower third of the state will be underwater by 2100." At the very least 120,000 oceanfront properties and fabulosity that is South Beach could be gone in several decades. No more Deco District. No more Hard Rock Stadium. No more empanadas. And like Emperor Nero fiddling while Rome burns, Florida has a state governor who prioritizes getting into fights with Disney, scrutinizing drag queens, and threatening the immigrant population the Florida economy depends on.

We may have gone past the point of no return in terms of climate change. When pondering this terrifying reality which might be approaching us faster than we could imagine, I have to make the conscious decision not to capitulate to the dark visions that could be approaching and keep a positive mindset. I have to choose to stay positive.

More electric cars such as Teslas seem to be filling Miami roads. Is it enough? Strides are being made in other countries to run on clean energy. Will we change in time? Will innovation and determination be enough to save the Magic City from vanishing? I know environmental groups are doing their best to tackle issues, but I also can't help but think, *where is the outrage?* When will people put down their phones, shout from the rooftops, and demand to be heard?

As for me, I'm undecided about my next step. How much longer I am going to antagonize the citizens of Miami with my struggle Spanish remains to be seen. With all the delicious food, I'm tempted to stay in South Florida. I recently got my first Florida driver's license, and for the first time, my picture is sort of flattering on the ID. In my California IDs, I usually end up looking like a swamp beast from the Everglades. Is it vain to consider living somewhere just because my ID finally looks good? OK, don't answer that. At any rate, it might be fun to live it up in South Florida while it still exists. Maybe I'll stay. Maybe I'll bounce. Maybe you'll have to meet me in Miami.

NOTES ON DATA COLLECTION

Though I have made more than 1,000 deliveries since coming to Miami, the data collection portion of the study was the 418 deliveries made in the Miami area from October 2022 through January 2023. At the time of writing, I have made a total of 1,008 deliveries throughout the Miami area for a total of $6,214.74.

About half the deliveries originated in the city of Miami Beach, but the delivery area took me as far west as Hialeah, as far north as Fort Lauderdale, and as far south as Pinecrest. During the data collection portion of the study, I attempted to accept every delivery that pinged me. I only declined deliveries if I needed a break or no parking was available.

The other 600 deliveries were not included in the statistics because after 418 deliveries I had to focus on making money and would skip low-ball delivery offers with no tip. Also, I would position my car in areas where it's easier to make money, which will weigh the statistics toward my delivery bias. Still, the other 600 deliveries helped inform my food recommendations and kept me financially afloat for the duration of the project.

When discussing the "Top 3" fast food establishments, it is worth noting that QSR reports them as 1. McDonald's 2. Starbucks 3. Subway 4. Taco Bell. In my research, I have categorized Starbucks as a cafe rather than a fast food; hence, I list the fast food establishments as McDonald's, Subway, and Taco Bell.

DISCLAIMERS

What you have been reading is what we writers like to call "creative nonfiction." Miami is such a cornucopia of crazy that the truth is much stranger than I could make up.

Recollections may vary, but each vignette contained herein is based on things I experienced, even if I obscured details to make people and places unidentifiable. Of course, when discussing the best restaurants and numerical data, I did my best to make it 100% accurate.

If you think you recognize yourself on these pages, I can assure you, it's definitely not you. Names, localities, and places have been obscured to protect the privacy of anyone I have met. Any similarities to actual persons, living or deceased, are just coincidences.

Everyone described in these pages is definitely (probably?) a "composite" character—that's when we writers take elements of several people we have met and blend them like a personality purée into one character. I'm soooo not talking about you whatsoever.

Facts and figures have been compiled to the best of my ability and double-checked and triple-checked. I barely remember any Algebra or Calculus, but I am a whiz at averaging tips and adding up totals in a spreadsheet. Who has time for long division? Did we need to learn that?

This work of creative nonfiction is not supported, endorsed, or funded by Uber, DoorDash, Postmates, TGI Friday's, or any other brand or corporation mentioned herein.

This publisher and author have made great efforts to present to you current and accurate information. We make no guarantee as to whether following any advice or strategy presented here will guarantee any results or success.

Please don't rub *espumita* all over your face and body. Unless you want to—like a pervert. It doesn't do anything. If it does, then L'Oreal can cut me a phat royalty check for all the Espumita Moisturizing Cream they're gonna sell for when you rub it all over yourself.

It pains me that I have to write this, but the telegram by Mary "the Minx" Brickell is merely a historical parody. The Spanish quote about Florida being filled with poisonous fruit and bogs, though, is from an actual historical source.

NONE of the photos in this book have been filtered, retouched, or Facetuned. They have merely been kissed by an angel and brushed by the seraphim.

ABOUT CHARLES ST. ANTHONY

Charles St. Anthony (Charles Ayres) has worked as a media personality in Japan and worked in Hollywood on shows such as *Lucifer*
and *Curb Your Enthusiasm*. He also appeared as one of the Tucka-
hoe Townsfolk in RuPaul's *The Bitch Who Stole Christmas*. So that's
something.

His humorous memoir *San Francisco Daddy* has acquired a cult following across the world, and his latest series of short reads on the gig economy has explored food while taking a snapshot of American culture in locales such as Beverly Hills, Oklahoma City, and now—of course—Miami.

Follow him on social media with the handle @kingcharles0921 on platforms such as Instagram and X. Then there is also the *T with Charles* podcast available on most major audio platforms.

FOOD ESTABLISHMENTS MENTIONED

Blue Collar (https://www.bluecollarmiami.com/)

6730 Biscayne Boulevard

Doggi's Arepa Bar (https://www.eatdoggis.com/)

7281 Biscayen Boulevard – Miami, FL

La Carreta (https://www.lacarreta.com/)

3632 SW 8th Street – Miami, FL

La Tiendita Taqueria (https://www.latienditataqueria.com/)

218 NW 25th Street – Miami, FL

Mi Colombia Cafeteria y Restaurante (https://www.yelp.com/biz/mi-colombia-cafeteria-y-restaurante-miami-beach)

701 71st Street – Miami Beach, FL

Mister01 (https://www.mister01.com/)

1680 Michigan Avenue – Miami Beach, FL

moshi moshi (https://moshimoshi.fun/)

1448 Washington Avenue – Miami Beach, FL

Spris Artisan Pizza (https://www.sprispizza.com/)

731 Lincoln Road – Miami Beach, FL

The Salty Donut (https://www.saltydonut.com/)

50 NW 24th Street – Miami, FL

Yambo (https://order.online/store/yambo-restaurant-miami-74766/)

1643 SW 1st St – Miami, FL

66

ACKNOWLEDGMENTS

First off, thank you to my husband, George. Te adoro. Te amo. Currently, George's country, Nicaragua, is experiencing immense turmoil. People do not have access to the food and medicine they need. Donate to help people in Nicaragua at https://www.christia-naid.org.uk/our-work/where-we-work/nicaragua.

Thank you to my longtime muse, editor, and friend, Marcella Hammer. You are amazing and your creative feedback is always genius. I'll give credit where credit is due—Marcella was instrumental in the discovery of the Mary "the Minx" Brickell telegram.

Special thanks to Krasnys for the editing. You can contact her at fiverr.com/krasnys.

Thank you to Will for the formatting wizardry and photo work. Find him fiverr.com/tlmason.

Should you need an infographic, Mujtaba is the best. Contact him at fiverr.com/mujtabaakhtar.

Did you see how cute my map of Miami was? Order a nice illustration from Fatima at fiverr.com/khushbofatima.

Once again, I thank all who contributed to GoFundMe for the creation of this book and to support my parents. This work would not exist without you, and I love you all!

Further, thanks go out to my longtime friend Apollo GT for hosting me upon my arrival in Florida. Check out his Apollo Male Models magazine at apollogt.com.

Thank you to my friends and fellow volunteers at the "Mar Vista Hostel." This project would not be possible without you.

Arigatou and kisses to Shimazu-san, Rocky, Cydonie, and Mayumi-san over at "Planet of Food." Watch the show (with appearances by yours truly) at youtube.com/@PlanetofFood3.

REFERENCES

Abad, Dylan. "Florida man charged for throwing hot dog at St. Pete officer." wfla.com. 3 July 2022. Retrieved 5 July 2022.

https://www.wfla.com/news/pinellas-county/florida-man-charged-for-throwing-hot-dog-at-st-pete-officer/.

Abad, Dylan. "Florida man drives stolen truck to Space Force base to warn of battle between aliens, dragons: reports." 25 July 2022. Retrieved 15 July 2023.

https://www.wfla.com/news/florida/florida-man-drives-stolen-truck-to-space-force-base-to-warn-of-aliens-dragons-reports-say/.

Anderson, Geoffrey. "The Best Restaurants in the Upper East Side." *Dish Miami*. 15 March 2023. Retrieved 13 July 2023, https://www.dish-miami.com/food-drink/best-restaurants-in-the-upper-east-side-miami/.

Barry, Dave. *Best. State. Ever. A Florida Man Defends His Homeland.* New York: G.P Putnam's Sons. 2016.

Balsera, Viviana Díaz and Rachel A. May, editors. *La Florida: Five Hundred Years of Hispanic Presence.* Gainesville, FL: University Press of Florida, 2014.

Becerra, Cesar A., *Orange Blossom 2.0.* Miami: Independently Published, 2021.

Bluebulb Project. The Measure of Things. Retrieved 14 July 2023. https://www.themeasureofthings.com/results.php?comp=length&unit=mi&amt=1177&p=2.

Clark, James C. *200 Quick Looks at Florida History.* Sarasota, Florida: Pineapple Press, Inc. 2000.

Fuson, Robert H. *Juan Ponce de Leon and the Spanish Discovery of Puerto Rico and Florida.* Blacksburg, Virginia: The McDonald & Woodward Publishing Company. 2000.

Luscombe, Richard. "Will Florida be lost forever to the climate crisis?" *The Guardian.* 21 April 2020. Retrieved 15 July 2020.

Marchante, Michelle. "Hey, Curious305: I don't want to wait at a drawbridge. When do they go up in Miami-Dade?" *The Miami Herald.* 19 February 2022. Retrieved 15 July 2023.

https://www.miamiherald.com/news/curious305/article258165073.html.

Plato. *Timaeus and Critias* (B Jowett, trans). Scotts Valley, CA: Independently Published, 2020.

"Ranking The (sic) Top 50 Fast Food Establishments in America." *QSR*. Retrieved 1 August 2023.

https://www.qsrmagazine.com/content/ranking-top-50-fast-food-chains-america/

Riess, Rebecca and Zoe Sottile. "79-year-old man hospitalized after alligator attack at Florida golf course community." *CNN*. 14 July 2023. Retrieved 15 July 2023.

https://www.cnn.com/2023/07/14/us/alligator-attack-naples-florida-trnd/index.html.

"Is Miami the best Florida city for your business?" *Florida Demographics*. 2023. Retrieved 9 July 2023.

https://www.florida-demographics.com/miami-demographics.

Peláez, Ana Sofia. *The Cuban Table: A Celebration of Food, Flavors, and History*. New York: St. Martins Press. 2014.

Sesín, Carmen. "Not Just Cubans: Many Latinos Now Call Miami Home." *NBC News*. 4 March 2014, Retrieved 9 July 2023, https://www.nbcnews.com/news/latino/not-just-cubans-many-latinos-now-call-miami-home-n37241.

Spencer, Terry. "Florida man threw live gator in Wendy's drive-thru window, police say." *Jacksonville.com*, 9 February 2016, Retrieved 15 July 2023,

https://www.jacksonville.com/story/news/2016/02/10/florida-man-threw-live-gator-wendys-drive-thru-window-police-say/985469007/.

Walters, Shamar. "John Balmer Arrested While Wearing 'I Have Drugs 'T-Shirt." *NBC News.* 7 January 2015. Retrieved 15 July 2023.

Wile, Rob. "Miami's biggest new wave of immigrants looks a lot like its previous ones." *Miami Herald*, 5 August 2019, Retrieved 9 July 2023, https://www.miamiherald.com/news/business/article232514327.html.

www.ingramcontent.com/pod-product-compliance
Lightning Source LLC
Chambersburg PA
CBHW040105150726
48005CB00013B/1579